PRAIRIE DOGS

LIVING WILD

Published by Creative Education and Creative Paperbacks
P.O. Box 227, Mankato, Minnesota 56002
Creative Education and Creative Paperbacks are imprints of The Creative Company
www.thecreativecompany.us

Design and production by Mary Herrmann
Art direction by Rita Marshall
Printed in China

Photographs by Alamy (Design Pics Inc.), Creative Commons Wikimedia (Cristinagil, Alan Hinkel, Leaflet, James Phelps, Anthony Quintano/Flickr, Joe Ravi, Nicholas A. Tonelli/Flickr, USFWS Mountain-Prairie/Flickr, zoo_attilly), Dreamstime (Andybignellphoto, Jiri Castka, Fischer0182, Miroslav Liska, Mikael Males, Scott Nelson, Nyker1, James Phelps Jr., Michael Tillotson, Robin Winkelman, Zrfphoto), Getty Images (fitopardo.com), iStockphoto (powerofforever, randimal), Shutterstock (AllaR15, Joseph M. Arseneau, Henk Bentlage, Rod Beverley, Roger Dale Calger, Marie Dirgova, Nick Fox, Zack Frank, Sandra Huber, I T A L O, Attila JANDI, l i g h t p o e t, Anh Luu, m_ grageda, Martha Marks, Marzolino, meunierd, poeticpenguin, Jaren Jai Wicklund, Kris Wiktor, Wollertz)

Library of Congress Cataloging-in-Publication Data
Names: Gish, Melissa, author.
Title: Prairie dogs / Melissa Gish.
Series: Living wild.
Includes bibliographical references and index.
Summary: A look at prairie dogs, including their habitats, physical characteristics such as their acrobatic movements, behaviors, relationships with humans, and the significance of their grassland burrows today.
Identifiers: LCCN 2016036685 / ISBN 978-1-60818-833-8 (hardcover) / ISBN 978-1-62832-436-5 (pbk) / ISBN 978-1-56660-881-7 (eBook)
Subjects: LCSH: Prairie dogs—Juvenile literature.
Classification: LCC QL737.R68 G57 2017 / DDC 599.36/7—dc23

CCSS: RI.5.1, 2, 3, 8; RST.6-8.1, 2, 5, 6, 8; RH.6-8.3, 4, 5, 6, 7, 8

First Edition HC 9 8 7 6 5 4 3 2 1
First Edition PBK 9 8 7 6 5 4 3 2 1

CREATIVE EDUCATION • CREATIVE PAPERBACKS

PRAIRIE DOGS

Melissa Gish

The sun is rising over the ponderosa pine-covered hills of South Dakota's Wind Cave National Park.

On the grassland below, black-tailed prairie dogs cautiously emerge from their burrows.

The sun is rising over the ponderosa pine–covered hills of South Dakota's Wind Cave National Park. On the grassland below, black-tailed prairie dogs cautiously emerge from their burrows. Sixweeks fescue and plains bluegrass quiver in the morning breeze, tempting the hungry animals. A mother and her four offspring rush to a nearby patch of fescue. They sit up on their hind legs and pull the slender grass toward their mouths, using their nimble forepaws to bend each blade. In the distance, bison rise from their slumber and begin grazing. A high-pitched call breaks through the calm air. The prairie dogs' lookout has spotted a red-tailed hawk overhead. The lookout barks continuously as the other prairie dogs race for their burrows. Then he, too, disappears underground. In a few minutes, when the threat has passed, the prairie dogs venture onto the grassland to continue their breakfast of tender, early-summer grass.

WHERE IN THE WORLD THEY LIVE

■ **Gunnison's Prairie Dog**
Utah, Colorado, New Mexico, and Arizona

■ **Utah Prairie Dog**
southwestern grasslands of Utah

■ **White-tailed Prairie Dog**
western Wyoming, western Colorado, eastern Utah, and southern Montana

■ **Black-tailed Prairie Dog**
from the Canadian border to the Mexican border

■ **Mexican Prairie Dog**
north-central Mexico

The five prairie dog species make their burrowing homes on the plains of North America. Although their wild populations are much smaller in modern times, their range still extends from Canada into Mexico. The colored squares represent common locations of each species found today.

Related to prairie dogs, the species of North American chipmunks tend to inhabit forested areas rather than plains.

F ound only in North America, prairie dogs were named *petits chiens*, or "little dogs," by early French explorers. The small **mammals** in the rodent order do not look anything like dogs. Rather, they earned this name from the yipping sound of their calls. Their closest relatives are ground squirrels, marmots, and chipmunks. Once, there were billions of prairie dogs living on the Great Plains from southern Canada to central Mexico. Since 1900, though, their numbers have been reduced by more than 90 percent.

The five prairie dog species look similar. They all have light brown fur and range from 12 to 15 inches (30.5–38.1 cm) in length. Some species are more bulky than others. Male prairie dogs of all species grow to be slightly bigger than females, but they lose weight during mating season. Prairie dogs are divided into two groups: those with white tail tips (Utah, Gunnison's, and white-tailed) and those with black tail tips (Mexican and black-tailed). The Utah prairie dog is the smallest species. It weighs between 1.5 and 2.5 pounds (0.7–1.1 kg). In 1973, the United States Fish and Wildlife Service

Prairie dogs follow a morning routine of stretching and sunning to prepare for a day of foraging and housekeeping.

Although their weight may drop by 50 percent, prairie dogs can survive up to six weeks without food or water during the summer.

listed this species as endangered, but today it is listed as threatened. Although 8,000 Utah prairie dogs exist in the southwestern grasslands of Utah, that number is falling. The Gunnison's prairie dog is found in the Four Corners region of the U.S. (where Utah, Colorado, New Mexico, and Arizona meet). This abundant species weighs no more than 2.5 pounds (1.1 kg) and lives at elevations of up to 10,000 feet (3,048 m). The white-tailed prairie dog also lives at such elevations. Its population is also abundant, and it inhabits western Wyoming and western Colorado as well as small areas of eastern Utah and southern Montana. White-tailed prairie dogs can weigh up to three pounds (1.4 kg).

The International Union for Conservation of Nature (IUCN) listed the Mexican prairie dog as endangered in 1990. This prairie dog is found only in north-central Mexico. It weighs up to 2.6 pounds (1.2 kg). Population data for the Mexican prairie dog is unclear, in part because this species is extremely rare. The black-tailed prairie dog ranges throughout the Plains, from the Canadian border to the Mexican border. About 1.5 million of them exist, though they are typically found in

Gunnison's prairie dogs live in the foothills of the Sangre de Cristo Mountains in southern Colorado and northern New Mexico.

Prairie dogs of all ages rely on touch and scent during greetings to learn about other members of their group.

abundance only in protected areas. Black-tailed prairie dogs weigh up to three pounds (1.4 kg).

Prairie dogs have short legs, with four digits on each front paw and five digits on each back paw. A dewclaw, located on the wrist of each front foot, is a remnant of prehistoric times and serves no purpose today. Long, sharp claws suited to digging in packed earth extend from each digit. Despite their stoutness, prairie dogs have powerful legs and can leap into the air and flip backwards. When threatened, prairie dogs race for their burrows at speeds of up to 35 miles (56.3 km) per hour. They are highly vocal animals; some species use a "language" of 12 different alarm calls that not only warn of predators but also give specific information about that predator.

Living on plains, prairie dogs are often subjected to high winds. And as burrowing animals, they are constantly throwing soil into their own faces. Nictitating (*NIK-tih-tayt-ing*) membranes (see-through inner eyelids) protect their eyes from dust and other particles. Prairie dogs have keen eyesight. The placement of the eyes on the sides of the head gives prairie dogs a wider range of

Prairie dogs constantly scan their surroundings, ever on the alert for approaching predators.

vision. It also enables them to distinguish the size, shape, and speed of a predator. Studies have revealed that prairie dogs have dichromatic vision, meaning they can see in blues, yellows, and some greens, but not reds.

Prairie dogs have very small ears set back far on their heads. This not only protects the ears from flying soil, but it also allows prairie dogs to pick up on sounds from all around. They rely on their sharp sense of hearing to detect predators and to hear the alarm calls of neighboring prairie dogs. The short, flattened tail is also used to communicate. Prairie dogs may cause their tails to flare (appear bushy) or quiver, a behavior called tail-flagging. Holding their tails high, straight out, or arched all signal certain types of information. Prairie dogs have very small noses, yet they are remarkably sensitive to smell. Scent is particularly important in social life, as prairie dogs use scent marking as a form of communication.

Glands in the prairie dogs' anal region emit musk, a greasy substance with an odor specific to each animal. They mark their territory by rubbing musk on rocks and plants, and they may even rub their musk on each other.

Each Utah prairie dog has variable markings, with some individuals having more black on their heads and bodies than others.

Encounters between unrelated prairie dogs of different social groups often involve chases or fights over territory.

This helps prairie dogs recognize each other and also signals when mating should take place. When prairie dogs are startled, they will scent-mark involuntarily. Because the scent is unpleasant to most other animals, this may be a form of defense that buys the prairie dog time to escape.

The three white-tailed species enter a period of torpor beginning in October or November. Torpor is a kind of temporary hibernation in which the muscles lock, body temperature drops, and the animal sleeps. During summer, these species add about 27 percent body fat, which sustains them through winter. About every eight days, the prairie dogs wake up and move around for about a day and a half—just long enough to raise their body temperature a little—and then they go back to sleep. The period of torpor lasts until February or March. Then the prairie dogs awaken in an angry mood. They fight with each other over territory for several weeks until all the territories are re-established. Black-tailed and Mexican prairie dogs do not hibernate. Instead, they grow a coat of dense underfur, usually by early November, which keeps them warm all winter. This underfur is shed in the spring.

University of Arizona studies have shown that fewer than one in five attempts by predators to capture a prairie dog is successful.

For safety, prairie dogs prefer treeless areas with vegetation less than 12 inches (30.5 cm) tall.

PRAIRIE DOG TOWN

Prairie dogs are in almost constant communication with each other, through greetings, scent, and vocal calls.

Prairie dogs may clip tall grass and plants around their burrows to create an unobstructed view of the area.

Prairie dogs live in communities called towns, where they dig extensive burrow systems. Each town consists of a number of territories. A territory might contain a single prairie dog, a male with several females, or several males and several females living together. Resident prairie dogs chase intruding prairie dogs out of their territory. If the town is in an area with an abundance of food, such as a dense grassland, the territories are typically held by single prairie dogs. In areas where food is scarce, territories are usually held by groups that share resources. Hidden underground, a town could have hundreds of prairie dogs and could sprawl across many acres.

Each burrow in a town has two or three funnel-shaped openings three to four inches (7.6–10.2 cm) in diameter. These openings lead to vertical shafts at opposite ends of the burrow system. The shafts vary from 6 to 16 feet (1.8–4.9 m) deep and connect to a system of tunnels. Near the surface are small rooms that allow prairie dogs to turn around quickly to exit the burrow. Deeper tunnels include separate sleeping and toilet areas.

Just as humans speak many different languages such as English, Arabic, and Japanese, each prairie dog species has its own language.

There is also a flood room that catches rainwater and helps keep the other rooms dry. The system of tunnels can be up to 100 feet (30.5 m) wide. Prairie dogs spend about half their day inside the burrow, resting and seeking shelter from the weather.

By digging burrows, prairie dogs help stimulate habitat growth. Burrows pull oxygen into the soil, spread **nutrients**, and provide pathways for rainwater to be absorbed into the ground. Many other animals also benefit from prairie dog burrows. Rabbits and snakes use them to escape the daytime heat. Burrowing owls do not dig their own burrows—they live mostly in prairie dog burrows. Even prairie dog predators such as swift foxes and black-footed ferrets use these burrows. And because prairie dogs are **herbivores**, many ground-nesting birds, feeling no threat from them, seek out their towns for nesting. In these grassland communities, insect prey are abundant, and the prairie dogs provide security for the birds, since their alarm calls warn of danger.

Prairie dogs employ a wide range of alarm calls to signal a threat. Each one is specific to a different predator, such as a coyote, hawk, dog, venomous snake, or even a

human. When prairie dogs encounter a perceived threat that they have never seen before, they create a new alarm call to describe it. A study conducted by Dr. Con Slobodchikoff of Northern Arizona University found that prairie dog calls indicate the type, size, shape, and even color of approaching predators. He recorded alarm calls and analyzed their patterns. He found that the alarm calls are made up of various units of sound, with each providing specific details. In this way, prairie dogs are using language, since each alarm call is constructed using these units, like words, to form a complete picture of the threat being described.

Scientists have discovered that snakes are the only predators for which prairie dogs produce a jump-yip.

Adults teach young prairie dogs how to communicate, including techniques of social grooming.

Other vocal communication includes social chatter. This occurs when a prairie dog lifts up its head and rattles off a string of calls, and then somewhere in the town another prairie dog lifts up its head and responds in a similar manner. The black-tailed and Mexican species engage in a behavior called the jump-yip. The prairie dog quickly stands up on its hind legs, stretches its front paws and face to the sky, and produces a sudden yipping call before dropping back to the ground. This behavior is performed in many contexts, from territorial disputes to the appearance or disappearance of a predator to excitement about mating.

All prairie dogs groom themselves, but only black-tailed prairie dogs maintain relationships by allogrooming, or grooming each other. Prairie dogs also engage in a bonding behavior called a greet-kiss. Two prairie dogs come up to each other, open their mouths, and touch their incisors together for a few seconds. Females greet-kiss each other and their young, called pups, and pups greet-kiss each other often. Adult males rarely greet-kiss except when a female initiates it—usually during mating season.

When a prairie dog is hibernating, its body curls up, its muscles become tense, and it cannot be unlocked from this position.

Males in search of mates are vulnerable to predators because their attention is focused on mating, not danger.

Utah prairie dogs have a black eyebrow mark above each eye, which distinguishes them from other prairie dog species.

Prairie dogs with black tail tips mate in January or February, and those with white tail tips mate in March or April. Sexual maturity varies. Some females are ready to mate at one year old. Others wait until their second year. Males are ready to mate between two and four years old. Mating season is a frantic time for prairie dogs, since females are fertile for only five hours each year. A female must mate with as many males as possible to ensure that she has a **genetically** diverse litter of pups. For this reason, during mating season, territory defense weakens because prairie dogs try to mate with as many partners from other territories as possible.

The female is pregnant for about 30 days. Then she gives birth inside a grass-lined nest chamber in her burrow. Typical litters consist of three to five pups, though up to eight are possible. Pups are born furless and blind. Their eyes open and their fur develops over a period of four to five weeks. At about six weeks of age, the pups venture aboveground with their mother and begin eating grass and plants. By eight weeks, they are completely **weaned**. The three white-tailed species remain with their mother throughout the summer and hibernate with her in the

winter. In the spring, they establish their own territory. The two black-tailed species leave their mother in the fall to establish their own territories before winter. Only half the pups born in a litter will survive their first year of life. Prairie dogs can live about eight years in the wild. However, with each passing year, a prairie dog's chance of survival is only about 50 percent.

Humans are the greatest threat to prairie dogs, but in the wild, coyotes are major predators. They may sneak into a town and grab prairie dogs that are far from their burrows, or they may lie down next to a burrow opening and wait for a prairie dog to emerge. Badgers also eat prairie dogs, invading burrows at night while prairie dogs are sleeping. Prairie dogs make up about 90 percent of the black-footed ferret's diet.

As long as littermates survive, they will continue to recognize each other for the rest of their lives.

A 19th-century scene of America's prairie was featured in Le Magasin Pittoresque, *a French publication of world discoveries.*

SHADOW CHASERS AND RAINMAKERS

P rairie dogs have long been symbols of the vastness of the American prairie and early settlers' desires to expand their boundaries west of the Mississippi. American explorer William Clark, traveling through what is now Nebraska in 1804, wrote in his journal about his crew's encounter with prairie dogs. On September 7, they killed one and cooked it for lunch. They then spent hours trying to flush the prairie dogs out of their burrows by pouring buckets of water into the holes. Finally, they captured one and took it as a traveling companion to their winter camp in North Dakota. In the spring, the prairie dog was sent to president Thomas Jefferson, who kept it as a pet.

Before people settled on a common name for them, prairie dogs were also called Louisiana marmots, prairie squirrels, barking squirrels, and mound yappers. Spanish settlers called them *perrito de la pradera*, meaning "little dog of the prairie." The Cherokee Indians called them *gili igodi ehi*. The Pawnee word for prairie dog is *wishtonwish*, the Zuni word is *tusa*, and the Lakota word is *pispiza*. Many American Indians respected the prairie dog for its

Prairie dogs share their habitat with many animals that pose no threat, including lizards, toads, and birds.

Prairie dogs may contract bubonic plague, a fatal disease carried by fleas, but a vaccine is being tested on prairie dogs in several states.

Like all rodents, prairie dogs have teeth that grow continuously and are worn down only by constant use.

Prairie dogs have 2 upper and 2 lower incisors for snipping off grass and plants and 18 cheek teeth for chewing.

ability to coexist peacefully with the many other animals on the prairie—especially the bison. And prairie dogs traditionally symbolized swiftness and preparedness.

It was also believed to be a magical creature that had power over rain. One story from the Jicarilla Apache tells how a terrible drought struck the land. A brave young man was sent in search of a rainmaker. He walked for many days with the heat of the sun beating down on him, but he could not find a rainmaker. Nearly dead from thirst, he fell down beside a prairie dog burrow. The prairie dog emerged and asked the man why he was there. The man told the prairie dog that he was searching for a rainmaker. The prairie dog gave the man a tiny cup of water. The man drank, but the cup never emptied. Then the prairie dog told the man to walk home. The man was so amazed by the bottomless cup that he put his faith in the prairie dog and walked home. When he got there, it was raining. This is why the Jicarilla Apache—and many other peoples—believe the prairie dog controls the rain.

Almost everyone has heard of Groundhog Day, which has been commemorated on February 2 every year since 1887. According to tradition, a groundhog from

Members of the Punxsutawney
Groundhog Club's Inner Circle
don top hats for the annual
Groundhog Day ceremony.

Pennsylvania named Punxsutawney Phil emerges from
his burrow to predict the weather. Seeing his shadow
foretells six more weeks of winter-like weather, but not
seeing his shadow means an early spring. However, Phil is
not the only rodent with forecasting powers: there's also
Prairie Dog Pete from Lubbock, Texas. On February 2,
Pete emerges from his burrow in a Lubbock prairie dog
town to similarly predict warm or cold weather.

Pete is the product of a conservation program that
began in 1935. In the early part of the 20th century,
prairie dogs were considered pests that competed for

7TH SEPTEMBER 1804

Septr. 7th Friday   A very Cold morning. Set out at daylight. We landed after proceeding 5 1/2 miles, near the foot of a round mounting which I saw yesterday resembling a dome. Capt. Lewis & my Self walked up, to the top which forms a Cone and is about 70 feet higher than the high lands around it, the Base is about 300 foot. In descending this Cupola, discovered a Village of Small animals that burrow in the ground (those animals are Called by the French Petite Chien). Killed one & Caught one alive by pouring a great quantity of water in his hole. We attempted to dig to the beds of one of those animals, after digging 6 feet, found by running a pole down that we were not half way to his Lodges, we found 2 frogs in the hole, and killed a Dark rattle Snake near with a Ground rat [*X: or prairie dog*] in him (those rats are numerous). The Village of those animals Covers about 4 acres of Ground on a Gradual descent of a hill and Contains great numbers of holes on the top of which those little animals Set erect make a Whistling noise and when alarmed Slip into their hole—we poured into one of the holes 5 barrels of water without filling it. Those Animals are about the Size of a Small Squirrel [*X: or larger, longer*] & thicker, the head much resembling a Squirrel in every respect, except the ears which is Shorter, his tail like a ground Squirrel which thy Shake & whistle when alarmed. The toe nails long, they have fine fur & the longer hair is gray.

From the journal of William Clark (1770-1838)

grassland with grazing livestock. The burrowing rodents were trapped, shot, and poisoned by the millions. Two Lubbock citizens, Mr. and Mrs. Kennedy N. Clapp, feeling concern for the survival of prairie dogs, established the first protected prairie dog town in a park in northeastern Lubbock. They started with four prairie dogs in two burrows in 1935. A year later, they began the tradition of commemorating Groundhog Day with Prairie Dog Pete as a stand-in for the groundhog Phil. The book *Our Comic Friend the Prairie Dog and the Story of Prairie Dog Town, Texas!* was published in 1973. Its authors, Frank Oliver and A. C. Hamilton, who was the director of the park at the time, recounted the Clapps' work and the success of the prairie dog town in attracting visitors from around the country. They also described the complex **ecosystem** of plants and animals sparked by the establishment of the prairie dog town.

Visitors to some of America's larger parks and monument sites on the Great Plains can see prairie dogs in their natural habitat. A prairie dog town sprawling roughly 40 acres (16.2 ha) is situated at the foot of Devils Tower. President Theodore Roosevelt proclaimed the

Devils Tower stands 1,267 feet (386 m) above the Belle Fourche River Valley; its base measures about 1,000 feet (305 m) around.

Visitors to South Dakota's Badlands National Park can stop by Roberts Prairie Dog Town to see hundreds of wild prairie dogs.

In areas where grass and tender plants are sparse, prairie dogs may dig for seeds, which provide many nutrients.

unique rock formation in northeastern Wyoming as America's first national monument in 1906. Roosevelt was an avid outdoorsman, hunter, and conservationist. Of his travels through prairie dog country, he wrote, "Around the prairie-dog towns it is always well to keep a look-out for the smaller carnivora, especially coyotes and badgers… and for the larger kinds of hawks. Rattlesnakes are quite plenty, living in the deserted holes, and the latter are also the homes of the little burrowing owls." Prairie dogs are also common from South Dakota's Black Hills National Forest to Big Bend National Park in Texas.

Most prairie dog towns cover less than half a square mile (1.3 sq km), but the largest recorded prairie dog town, once located in Texas, was much bigger. It covered roughly 25,000 square miles (64,750 sq km) and was home to as many as 400 million prairie dogs. A biologist named Vernon Bailey first recorded the site in 1902. Since the 1950s, two prairie dogs have been competing for another world record. On the outskirts of the small town of Oakley, Kansas, sits an enormous 8,000-pound (3,629 kg) concrete statue of a prairie dog. Standing 15 feet (4.6 m) tall, it boasts of being the world's largest

Wyoming's shortgrass prairie ecosystem supports a chain of life, from the smallest insects to the biggest grazing mammals.

prairie dog. However, another concrete prairie dog stands as part of the Ranch Store attraction in Cactus Flats, South Dakota. This one weighs 12,000 pounds (5,443 kg) and stands 12 feet (3.7 m) tall. It, too, advertises itself as the world's largest prairie dog. The Kansas prairie dog is taller, while the South Dakota prairie dog is heavier. It is left up to visitors to decide which of the two should rightfully be dubbed "largest."

At the height of summer, wildflower stems and leaves provide much-needed nutrition as well as moisture.

KEEPERS OF THE GRASSLAND

The success of bison herds was historically tied to the success of prairie dog towns across the Great Plains.

The first prairie dogs did not appear on Earth until about two and a half million years ago. Very few fossils of early prairie dogs exist—most are jaws and skulls of a creature that **evolved** much later into the five species of prairie dogs known today. The first Gunnison's prairie dog on record existed about 750,000 years ago in southern Colorado. About 500,000 years ago, a white-tailed species called *Cynomys niobrarius* emerged. Roughly 375,000 years later, it evolved into the modern white-tailed and Utah prairie dogs. The first black-tailed prairie dogs appeared about 75,000 years ago. About 42,000 years ago, some of these black-tailed prairie dogs branched off to become Mexican prairie dogs.

For thousands of years, prairie dogs have been a keystone species, which means they are vital to the success of an ecosystem. More than 200 animals and countless **invertebrates** live in the ecosystem of a prairie dog town. A keystone species is irreplaceable—when it declines, other animals that are dependent on the habitat also decline. Prairie dogs not only coexist with other

Captive prairie dogs will eat many foods linked to a human diet, such as root vegetables, fruits, and even cooked chicken.

Black-tailed prairie dogs eat a variety of vegetation, but Mexican prairie dogs tend to stick with one type of grass and one type of plant.

animals on the prairie, but they also help shape and maintain the landscape for their neighbors.

On dry, windswept prairies, soil erosion is a problem. Without grass to anchor the dirt, wind carries away precious topsoil. And since the soil is fine-grained and hard-packed, rainwater runs off, taking even more topsoil. But prairie dogs encourage the growth of grass and plants that hold soil in place, and their burrows act as **aquifers** that allow water to travel deep into the soil. Prairie dogs' digging increases the oxygen in the soil and loosens dirt, allowing a variety of flowering grasses and plants to seed down and grow. Prairie dogs are responsible for turning and fertilizing nearly 12,000 pounds (5,443 kg) of soil per acre (0.4 ha)—more than 8 times that of all other burrowing animals in a prairie habitat.

Prairie dogs keep the vegetation around their burrows clipped, increasing protein, nitrogen, and moisture in the plants and grasses. Animals that eat this vegetation— pronghorn, elk, and bison—get more nutrients, so their health and populations increase. Other small herbivores such as rabbits, kangaroo rats, mice, and ground squirrels also increase, providing food for carnivores such as

Thunder Basin National Grassland in Wyoming is home to the largest population of black-tailed prairie dogs in the world.

Nearly 1,300 bison share 71,000 acres (28,733 ha) of grassland with prairie dogs in South Dakota's Custer State Park.

coyotes, badgers, burrowing owls, and hawks. More flowering plants attract butterflies, grasshoppers, and other insects that feed toads and birds such as horned larks, prairie chickens, and grouse. Without prairie dogs, all these plants and animals would disappear.

For thousands of years before European settlers moved across the Mississippi River, about 30 billion prairie dogs coexisted with roughly 60 million bison throughout the Great Plains. When cattle, horses, and sheep were introduced to the Plains in the 19th century—and began overgrazing—ranchers saw the prairie dogs not as stewards of the prairie but as unwelcome competitors. Wrongly convinced that prairie dogs were eating all the vegetation and that livestock were breaking their legs by stepping in prairie dog burrows, ranchers waged war on prairie dogs. They trapped, shot, and poisoned the animals, but prairie dogs were not disappearing fast enough to suit ranchers.

In 1915, the U.S. government funded a widespread campaign to eradicate prairie dogs. Pellets laced with nerve **toxin** were dropped into burrows. The pellets killed not only prairie dogs but also many other small animals and birds. Within 50 to 60 years, prairie dogs were wiped out from 98 percent of their former range. The loss of prairie dogs also resulted in the near–**extinction** of black-footed ferrets. And without prairie dogs to encourage the growth of nutritious plants and grasses, shrubs and toxic weeds spread across the prairies. The land no longer supported the livestock that it had been altered for. Entire prairie ecosystems collapsed.

While less widespread today, government programs to poison prairie dogs still exist. In addition, prairie dog hunting has become a popular sport. Of the 30 billion prairie dogs once inhabiting North America, fewer than 2 million exist today. Conservation biologists who recognize the need for prairie dogs to rebuild ecosystems are working

Prairie dogs are essential to the survival of black-footed ferrets, also known as American polecats.

The Chihuahuan Desert, stretching from southeastern Arizona to north-central Mexico, is North America's second-largest desert.

In 2007, landowners agreed to help the conservation group Pronatura Noroeste protect 42,000 acres (16,997 ha) of Mexican prairie dog habitat.

at reintroducing prairie dogs to some of their former ranges. Wildlife biologist Dr. Ana Davidson was part of a team that reintroduced more than 1,000 Gunnison's prairie dogs to a grassland ecosystem in central New Mexico and then studied them for 8 years. When the study concluded in 2014, Davidson reported that global **climate change** leading to drought severely limited the prairie dogs' ability to re-establish in New Mexico.

Dr. Gerardo Ceballos, a **behavioral ecologist** at the National Autonomous University of Mexico, has had greater success with Mexican prairie dogs. In the late 1980s, Dr. Ceballos began working to rebuild a prairie ecosystem in an area of Chihuahua, Mexico, that was once home to prairie dogs. In desert habitats, a shrub called mesquite can overtake a grassland prairie and destroy it, turning it into a dry scrubland. But prairie dogs kill mesquite, making way for grass and plants to grow. When a team of researchers led by Dr. Ceballos reintroduced Mexican prairie dogs into an area of scrubland, it took only one year for the prairie dogs to remove all the mesquite and turn the land back into a healthy prairie. In 2001, Dr. Ceballos's team successfully reintroduced black-footed ferrets to the prairie as well.

Because of Ceballos's work, the Mexican government established the Janos Biosphere Reserve in December 2009. The first of its kind in Mexico, the reserve is dedicated to the preservation of 1.3 million acres (526,091 ha) of native grassland habitat. Ceballos's team has been working to bring pronghorn, desert bighorn sheep, wolves, and even bison back to the prairie. In 2009, a herd of 23 bison from Wind Cave National Park in South Dakota was donated to the Janos Biosphere Reserve, where they coexist with the now firmly established population of Mexican prairie dogs. Such conservation efforts are necessary all across the Great Plains of North America if prairie dogs are to reclaim and secure their role as keepers of the grassland for generations to come.

Mexican prairie dogs are content to share their burrows with spotted ground squirrels and burrowing owls.

ANIMAL TALE: THE FOOLISH PRAIRIE DOGS

Prairie dogs traditionally play secondary roles in American Indian stories. This tale has a shared history among several Great Plains tribes. It depicts prairie dogs as the subjects of a trick played by the skunk and the coyote as they try to get an easy meal.

Coyote had traveled a long way without food. He was so weak from hunger that he fell down at the edge of the prairie dog town. He did not have the energy to chase the prairie dogs. Skunk happened by and saw Coyote. "I have a plan to help you get those prairie dogs without lifting a paw," he told Coyote.

"How?" asked Coyote.

"You play dead, and I will tell the prairie dogs," instructed Skunk.

Coyote wasn't sure how this would help him get the prairie dogs, but he did as Skunk said. Then Skunk ran into the prairie dog town and announced Coyote's demise. "Let's celebrate," he told the prairie dogs. "You will never have to fear Coyote again! Bring a drum and follow me."

The prairie dogs were thrilled. They followed Skunk to the edge of their town, and there they saw Coyote. He appeared quite dead. His eyes were closed, and he was motionless.

"Come dance in a circle around Coyote," Skunk told the prairie dogs, taking their drum. "We will celebrate the passing of his spirit and the safety of your town."

And so all the prairie dogs did as Skunk told them. They formed a circle around Coyote and joined hands. Skunk stood beside Coyote and beat the drum. The prairie dogs danced.

"Now close your eyes," Skunk said. "Coyote's spirit is about to pass. If you open your eyes, you will see Coyote's ghost, and that will be a bad thing."

The prairie dogs were afraid to see Coyote's ghost, so they closed their eyes. Skunk continued to beat the drum, and the prairie dogs continued to dance. Then Skunk nudged Coyote. Coyote got to his feet and grabbed a prairie dog. With one bite, the prairie dog was killed. He grabbed another and another as fast as he could.

The prairie dogs stopped dancing. Coyote dropped to the ground to play dead again. "What was that noise?" one of the prairie dogs asked. He opened his eyes and saw his companions lying dead next to Coyote. "What happened?" he cried. All the prairie dogs looked.

"You see," Skunk said, "they opened their eyes and saw Coyote's ghost." The prairie dogs were terrified.

"No more dancing," they said. "We want to go home." The prairie dogs took their drum and ran back to their town.

Coyote stood up and laughed. "That was a good trick," he told Skunk. He gathered up all the fat prairie dogs he had killed and carried them away from the prairie dog town with Skunk close behind.

"Where are you going?" Skunk called out. "Aren't you going to share?"

"I don't think so," said Coyote.

"Wait," called Skunk, "I will cook them for you." Coyote stopped and turned to Skunk. "You go get some wood for a fire," Skunk told him, "and I will cook them."

So Coyote dropped the prairie dogs and went off to find firewood. Skunk scooped up all but one prairie dog and ran off into the dark. When Coyote returned, he found that the prairie dogs had not been the only ones tricked by Skunk.

GLOSSARY

aquifers – pockets of water deep below ground, often tapped for drinking water and crop irrigation

behavioral ecologist – a scientist who studies the effects of environmental pressures on the behavior of animals

climate change – any long-term change of pattern in the planet's or a region's atmosphere, environments, and long-term weather conditions

ecosystem – a community of organisms that live together in an environment

evolved – gradually developed into a new form

extinction – the act or process of becoming extinct; coming to an end or dying out

genetically – relating to genes, the basic physical units of heredity

glands – organs in a human or animal body that produce chemical substances used by other parts of the body

herbivores – animals that eat primarily grass and plants

invertebrates – animals that lack a backbone, including spiders, insects, and worms

mammals – warm-blooded animals that have a backbone and hair or fur, give birth to live young, and produce milk to feed their young

nutrients – substances that give an animal energy and help it grow

toxin – a substance that is harmful or poisonous

vaccine – a substance given to provide protection from a disease

weaned – made the young of a mammal accept food other than nursing milk

SELECTED BIBLIOGRAPHY

Graves, Russell A. *The Prairie Dog: Sentinel of the Plains*. Lubbock: Texas Tech University Press, 2001.

Humane Society of the United States. "Prairie Dog Status Report." Prairie Dog Coalition. http://www.humanesociety .org/about/departments/prairie_dog_coalition/prairie -dog-species-status.html.

Johnsgard, Paul A. *Prairie Dog Empire: A Saga of the Shortgrass Prairie*. Lincoln: University of Nebraska Press, 2005.

National Geographic. "Prairie Dog: *Cynomys ludovicianus*." http://animals.nationalgeographic.com/animals/mammals /prairie-dog.

Shefferly, Nancy. University of Michigan Museum of Zoology. "*Cynomys ludovicianus*: Black-tailed Prairie Dog." Animal Diversity Web. http://animaldiversity.org/accounts /Cynomys_ludovicianus.

Slobodchikoff, C. N., Bianca S. Perla, and Jennifer L. Verdolin. *Prairie Dogs: Communication and Community in an Animal Society*. Cambridge, Mass.: Harvard University Press, 2009.

Note: Every effort has been made to ensure that any websites listed above were active at the time of publication. However, because of the nature of the Internet, it is impossible to guarantee that these sites will remain active indefinitely or that their contents will not be altered.

As prairie dogs continue to reclaim their historic range, visitors to wilderness areas will be able to enjoy these observant animals.

INDEX